MW00935449

# Way to Go

*A research-based strategy for establishing a positive relationship between parents and teachers*

MARY BETH GAERTNER, ED.D.

authorHOUSE®

AuthorHouse™
1663 Liberty Drive
Bloomington, IN 47403
www.authorhouse.com
Phone: 1-800-839-8640

First published by AuthorHouse 3/31/2011

ISBN: 978-1-4567-3640-8 (e)
ISBN: 978-1-4567-3642-2 (sc)

Library of Congress Control Number: 2011903747

Printed in the United States of America

# Dedication

*This book is dedicated to the teachers past and present of Salem Lutheran School. They have taught me what focus and persistence are all about and how much sacrifice is involved in educating children. They have been truly Called to serve.*

*May God bless you all!*

# Contents

*TELL Lead as the professional! In the
educational arena, the teacher is the professional.
If schools were hospitals, teachers would be the
doctors. They would be diagnosing, treating,
adjusting, monitoring progress, etc. Indeed,
teachers are the professionals.*

*Conclusions*

# Foreward

**H**ave you ever set out on a journey without a destination in mind? Not merely a Sunday drive or a hike in the woods, but rather a journey or a long vacation? I would guess that the answer for most of us would be no. Vacations and travel take careful planning. Destinations are researched. Reservations are made. Much preparation takes place. We must choose which WAY TO GO! As teachers we prepare for the new school year, our own professional journey, with vigor. We hang bulletin boards and plan curriculum, but how much time do we put into researching our destination? How much do we specifically prepare for the individual students we will be teaching for the next year?

When Mary Beth shared that she wanted to write a book about our experiences with the "Tell the Teacher More Days," I knew what she had to name it. Anyone who knows her knows that her enthusiasm is infectious! Her chant "WAY TO GO!" can be heard throughout the hallways as she cheers on the teachers, students, and even the parents of our school. She sets the positive tone of our school and guides us to our own destination.

As a teacher on her staff I have participated in the "Tell the Teacher More Days" and believe it is the WAY TO GO!

This past fall, not a month after school began, I found myself sitting in the hospital as my husband awaited emergency surgery to remove his gallbladder. I sent off a quick email to the kindergarten parents letting them know I would likely be out for a few days and why. I could never have imagined all the kind responses I received form the parents.

One parent worked at the hospital and stopped by to see us right before surgery. Another parent served on the Board of the hospital and asked the hospital chaplain to stop in for a prayer. All in just a few hours! To feel surrounded and supported by Salem parents in this troubling time was amazing.

I believe making that initial connection at the beginning of the year with "Tell the Teacher More Days" made their warm responses possible. Relationships had been formed. There was a familiarity that would have taken much longer to create had we not had those "Tell the Teacher More" meetings. For an educator looking to make the awkward "getting to know you" phase of the first few weeks of school a thing of the past, the model you will read about in this book is the WAY TO GO! It is the way to form a partnership with parents before school starts and the way to gain understanding about each of the special students in your class. This model begins a journey, envisions a destination and guides you on the WAY TO GO!

### *Blessings on your journey- Kim Chaisson*
*Kindergarten Teacher, Salem Lutheran School*

# Introduction

Writing a book was never one of my personal goals or aspirations. Sharing something that really works with other educators for the betterment of schools is! So, in order to share the success of this method of positive communication between teachers and parents to the widest audience possible, writing a book is the WAY TO GO!

Perhaps the two most difficult constituencies to convince about anything new are teachers and parents. Maybe that's because we all have had experience with parents –and with schools! Or we all think we are experts due to our experience? Fact is, we are coming at the topic from personal experience and therefore, personal points of view.

So much research has been done on the qualities of successful schools. Almost all of the research about successful schools rates the involvement of parents to be a critical factor. Our school is no different- we have a very high rate of involvement from our parents. In fact, we track our parent volunteer hours each year and the average is about 11,000 hours per school year. Yet, we still have issues with parents not sharing their expectations or worse, the school not meeting their expectations for their child. We still have teachers who have difficulty sharing concerns they have about their students. We may have all the educational accolades and awards, but how we communicate is still the necessary and sometimes missing ingredient in meeting expectations.

In my nearly thirty years of educational travels, I specifically remember one of my psychology professors making the point about what determines a problem.

He said the difference between the expectation and the reality constitutes the problem. So, if you have a parent that never voiced the expectation, and a teacher who is skeptical or even a bit frightened about sharing the reality of how the student is achieving or behaving, we really do have a problem- a big one! We have always been known as a very caring school – one that treats students with love and respect. The problem comes in when we as a school aren't coming across as clearly as we should or when things aren't humming along and perfectly as a parent may expect. We need to change both the expectation and the reality. If the way we are currently doing things isn't improving, then why are we continuing to do the same thing? Let's find a better WAY TO GO!

Please don't think this is the one and only to answer to your communication issues! There are many things we have done to help us to both lay out our expectations and the way in which we deliver the realities. All involve data - and for both parents and teachers, the data speaks for itself. We survey our school community fairly often to determine their expectations and then we survey again to see how well we are meeting them. Thus, when we took on "Tell the Teacher

More Day," it was only logical to use the data to see if it made a difference!

The positive feedback from the data has provided both parents and teachers a much needed avenue from which to springboard their year in terms of communication with each other. The comments from the teachers are verbatim and the emails shared between parents and teachers are authentic. Therefore, other than removing names, editing within them has not occurred.

WAY TO GO will provide the philosophy and the educational research behind the strategy for the positive communication model, the necessary ingredients for the successful implementation of "Tell the Teacher More Day" as well as the follow through, and the actual quotations, including emails between parent and teacher, from the teachers themselves who are the front lines in parent communication. I consider the teacher comments to be like gold. The comments are solid, sincere and shining from those who know the students best! Now we have a WAY TO GO in how to best communicate what we have to say to the parents.

I invite you to implement "Tell the Teacher More Day" and replicate the research to make it your own!

*Dr. Mary Beth Gaertner*

# Acknowledgements

Without the discovery of the article written by *Richard Schumacher, Jr.*, this book would not be written. It was the discovery of his theory that motivated me to take it on as a project in our own school. Always believing that people like to do business with people they like, this article made so much sense! We had a dedicated, professional faculty who I believed to be up to the challenge.

Then, the across my desk the next spring came the book from the Master Teacher, *Robert DeBruyn*. This is a little book with a mighty impact! After a successful first year of "Tell the Teacher More Day," I felt we were ready to embrace the book's very practical advice on working with parents after we had established the initial introduction. Wow! What powerful how-to's in dealing with tough issues. DeBruyn is candid in making the point that since the teacher is the professional in the teacher-parent relationship, the teacher is therefore responsible for the communication – whether it is positive or not. Parents want information, good or bad.

If we already had established a good relationship with parents, then taking the next steps to communicate effectively using concepts from DeBruyn's book seemed the WAY TO GO! I will admit that only Divine intervention made all of this come together. It is with *all glory to God* that I give my greatest acknowledgement. It is indeed my sincere desire that schools take hold of these concepts and use them for the sake of their students' future growth and success!

# Chapter One

*Is there anything out there that can help us to communicate more effectively with parents?*

Nothing concerns me more as a school administrator or causes me more angst as the fear of unhappy parents. Very early in my career as an early childhood administrator, I vividly remember a mommy physically backing me up to the wall with her jabbing words and bullying attitude. It seemed there had to be more going on than her discontent with a teacher who "wasn't loving enough" toward her child. I clearly remember her saying to me while I was literally up against the wall in my office "Don't you want to hit me?" That's when I knew there was something clearly wrong with this picture. I had to figure out how not to get into this situation or one like it ever again. I was defenseless and appeared weak by not responding to her threats and taunting. She calmed down when I wouldn't respond. So, first thing I learned – diffuse anger by listening and staying calm.

My deeper concern was how to prevent a parent from

getting this angry in the first place. In my attempt to get to the root of the problem and to please this mommy, I talked with the daddy. He assured me that when it comes to her child she easily gets upset. What a shock to find out he was a lawyer! Was she taunting me to get a lawsuit?

My goodness, this situation was becoming even more difficult to resolve by the moment. There had to be a way to prevent this from happening again. Years went by as together the teachers and I took workshops, read books, collaborated about our concerns with whom we termed "difficult parents." Most of us if not all of us were also parents as well as educators. We knew how important a child's welfare and educational experience is to the parent. Steven A. Kaatz (DeBruyn, 1999) writes "A special danger in Lutheran schools is that some parents expect perfect children in perfect rows behaving perfectly. There may be an honest disconnect between what the parent expects of school personnel and what the school personnel expects of themselves. What the parent really wants is an educator who has a personal touch and who is 'authentic.'" Jane Henderson (DeBruyn, 1986) writes in her research that "for the truly unreasonable parent, there is no easy answer. It is helpful to remember that what might be perceived as unreasonableness, may actually be fear and lack of trust in school people, or in institutions in general. Non-defensiveness and calm on your part can go a long way in calming that parent down."

Being a private school, pleasing parents is compounded because we know parents have a choice as to where they place their child for a formal education. Years came and went. We employed various strategies to help with difficult parents and attempts to be proactive. We held parent conferences and parent orientations to discuss the importance of going to the teacher at the first sign of concern to help keep the lines of communication open.

We drafted policies and followed procedures within our policy handbooks and parent agreements that had to be signed by all parents. We still had occasional issues and were always looking for another strategy to help us become more proactive and confident in dealing with our parents – a strategy we could all use consistently and depend upon for communicating with parents.

As a faculty and staff we determined that should a parent come to us with a concern or questions regarding another teacher and their child, we would listen to the parental concern but always redirect the parent back to the teacher in question. (A biblical truth for those of you in Christian schools - Matthew 18.) Going to the teacher directly involved was also the most efficient way to retrieve "eye witness" information concerning the topic and situation. Sometimes the parent would follow the advice and other times would not, whether out of fear of being thought to be too trivial or confrontational or that retribution would be taken out on their child. As faculty, staff and administrators, we would go to that specific teacher and provide an "fyi" so that he or she would be informed that something was becoming a problem. In this way, he or she would be prepared to deal with the parental concern appropriately without being caught off guard. When a faculty and staff trust one another this scenario works well. If on the other hand, there is distrust or when the faculty and staff members are new to this process, it can be a complication for implementing this strategy.

Parents were learning to follow the policy and procedures and when they didn't, they were reminded to do so. We emphasized the strategy to new school families and how important it was to partner effectively to achieve good communication between the home and the school. So, the strategy seemed to be working well and something was finally in place to deal with difficult parents. We determined this to be the best avenue so far. We decided to let it work for us.

One particular situation still reminds me of how passionate a parent can become over the education of their child. Rather than being discontent with a situation within the classroom, this parent was very unhappy with the way the administration handled a situation with teachers. Two teachers were discovered to be having an inappropriate relationship. Both teachers were relieved of their teaching duties. Families were informed and students were counseled. Not to our surprise, not everyone agreed with our decision.

One parent in particular blew into my office and offered "How much will it take to keep (the teacher)?" It seemed only what mattered was this teacher teaching this child. After I restated the offer in my own words and then gently declined the offer, he became irate. He threatened a lawsuit and to take the situation to the highest authority. That he did. The offer was declined again. A letter from his attorney soon followed requesting any and all monetary and nonmonetary items that had been donated by the family to be returned. For obvious reasons, that could not happen.

When the parent had no legal recourse, parking lot conversations began to spring up and a campaign to pit the administration against the parents to get the teachers back developed. Here we go again- that urging desire for a proactive strategy to handle the difficult parents!

I will share two more scenarios concerning situations with parents to help you realize that you are not alone with these types of concerns and in a search for a proactive strategy that works to prevent them from occurring, or at least to help to keep a handle on things if the situation tends to get out of control. Each year for three consecutive years, the parent ends up "telling off" the teacher in person, on the phone, or via email, because the parent feels that the child is being held responsible for something he did not do or that he is being misunderstood, or that classroom issues are not being handled correctly. It seems that the child's perspective is the correct one and the one that needs attention. Through this particular ongoing scenario, we learned that if a parent's issue isn't resolved the first time, it only accumulates and will get worse as time goes by.

I can still remember the many one on one conversations I had with the three teachers involved with this parent. We did our professional best to stand our ground and help this parent understand the truth of the whole situation rather than to depend on just the child's point of view.

New teacher, seasoned teacher, it didn't matter. Staying calm and listening was the only option. Eventually, it paid off when, at the teacher's invitation, the parent saw with their own eyes the child's behavior. Again, how could this have been prevented in the first place? (Actual emails will be shared with you later under strategies so that you can glean best practices and hopefully be on your game should this type of situation arise for you.)

One last example involves the gossiping parent. When your school is a school of choice, word of mouth either sells or ruins a school's reputation and that always affects enrollment. It happened that a student made an inappropriate comment. Another child made the good choice of reporting it to the teacher. The teacher properly reported the incident to the parents and disciplined the student involved. While the disciplinary situation was well under control by the teacher, another parent took it upon herself to contact other parents and inform them of her personal take on the matter, even to the point of sharing her opinion with a new parent to the system who felt it all to be unsolicited and very disconcerting. The gossip? It went on for weeks. What can we do to be proactive in communication with difficult parents?

From the teacher and administrator's perspective, the fear of having to confront a parent due to the lack of progress, less than acceptable behavior or otherwise gets in the way of good communication.

One of our kindergarten teachers shared with me that she was so concerned about a parent's attitude toward her that she couldn't focus clearly and the concern was "sucking the joy" out of her teaching the children! This comment came from a confident teacher that has been teaching for over fifteen years! So, both teachers and parents have much to learn about communicating for a win-win situation. It just shouldn't have to be this hard.

# Chapter Two

*The Discovery of the Positive Communication Theory*

**A**s faculty, staff and administrators, we are advocating and practicing that when we get "backed to the wall, we will remain calm and not become defensive." (You already know where that came from.) It never fails that when one of us becomes defensive, the parent interprets it as not listening or not caring. While I think we are better off than in years past, miscommunication still happens and we keep searching for strategies to help us become better at our communication skills.

Two summers ago, while reading my educational journals, *I came across an interesting article written by Richard W. Schumacher, Jr., a professor at Concordia University, Ann Arbor, Michigan. It was entitled "Bridging the Communication Gap: The Value of Intentional Positive Teacher-Initiated Communication."* Having been an educator and an administrator, he was seeking a process by which to ease the tensions of both parents and teachers to find a common ground on which to communicate comfortably. His theory suggests that a gap exists between parents and teachers and that they will communicate in one of two ways: individually or collaboratively.

Attempts at one sided communication result in a number of negative outcomes, not limited to:

Accusations against one another

Assumptions replacing facts in decision making

Avoidance of one another to reduce conflict

Defensiveness against what others might be saying

Gossip designed to gain a body of support against the other party

Lack of information, which leads to assumptions and inaccuracy

Lack of support —both real and perceived

Misinformation that becomes an almost uncorrectable truth

On the other hand, he postulates that collaborative communication between parents and teachers will produce positive outcomes:

Accurate information shared by both parents and teachers

Both parties gain confidence in the abilities of each other

Both parties make collaboration a priority

Rapport grows between parents and teachers, making communication easier and more effective

Mutual support between home and school is fostered.

Schumacher's theory places the responsibility for the collaboration upon the school. He writes that the school needs to initiate the communication and it must be positive. To interject some humor and understanding here, Schumacher writes "…parents already have an expectation that the school will contact them when their child is misbehaving or has fallen behind. In fact, that expectation is so strong that, for many parents, the appearance of the teacher's name on their caller ID is grounds for an immediate elevation of their heart rate."

## Research Review of the Positive Communication Theory

*Schumacher's literature review of the impact of parent involvement only added more credibility to what we as a school were experiencing.* "Parent's overall evaluations of the teacher, their sense of comfort with the school, and their reported level of involvement was higher when they received frequent and effective communications" (Ames de Stefano, Watkins, and Sheldon, 1995). The same research also shows that the way teachers use communication tools is dependent upon their pre-conceived attitudes and beliefs. Freytag's research (2001) revealed that parents want to hear positive as well as negative news concerning their children. My mentor at Sam Houston State University in the late 1980's and author, Dr. Laverne Warner, found that "teachers should be encouraged to personalize their communications to parents in order to give it a friendlier and less rigid tone."

Research by Upham, Cheney, and Manning in 1998 revealed that both parents and teachers agree meeting in person to discuss issues one-on-one in an in-depth manner is preferable to a phone call or sending a note. Both groups also agreed that although it was difficult to fit in meetings at the start of school year, it was best to do so. Teachers preferred a large group meeting, while parents favored one-on-one meetings where their child's unique needs could be discussed privately. Witmer (2005) stated that starting the school year out with strong lines of communication will pay dividends for the student and the school community. Barrera and Warner (2006) determined that schools must also work to be intentional in the development of a method to address the unique needs of each of their families.

## The Birth of Parents Day

*Schumacher developed this vehicle out of a conversation with another educator.* Fifteen minute increments were assigned for teachers to meet with parents. Teachers listened and parents talked. Besides learning about the students, best communication methods to follow between parents and teachers were determined. Schumacher discussed the sales job necessary to get both teachers and parents on board for this day. His surveys of parents afterward as to the success of the day bore out the positive impact.

## Praise God! We found it!

*It is here that I decided to give this a try.* I called Mr. Schumacher and asked permission to replicate the idea as well as the follow up survey. I humorously said that if this works we need to write a book about it to help everyone out there that needs a method to develop positive communication between school and home! I shared Schumacher's article with the faculty and developed a one page form for parents to complete and bring with them to the fifteen minute appointments for which they signed up. The form we used is included in Chapter Five, Tell the Teacher More Day.

# Chapter Three

*Who are we? Two very different schools yield very similar results.*

As I write this, it is the end of the first semester and our school has completed "Tell the Teacher More Day" for the second year in a row. I am convinced more than ever this method works. In this chapter, I hope to share with you the various demographics of our two schools, along with the specific research we developed. With online surveys it makes participation by school families simple and fast. The results can be tallied and analyzed quickly. You will want to know if your families agree that the time was well spent and led to satisfaction in terms of positive communication.

I also want to share with you some actual emails exchanged between parents and educators as the year progressed to demonstrate the open communication that developed from "Tell the Teacher More Day." I would not want you to think that everything is perfect- we certainly experienced our share of negative communication. Both parents and teachers work to be clear and to work toward understanding. We believe that as the educators we are indeed the professionals. It is up to us to follow up to be certain the issues are dealt with in a positive, caring manner. Contrary to what some of us might want to believe, things don't go away if we ignore them!

Finally, I will share with you the comments from our teachers. These comments will include those concerning "Tell the Teacher More Day" as well as the impact that the day had on communication throughout the year. Perhaps the most difficult and hardest people to convince about trying something new, is a group of experienced educators. Nothing proves a point like real data!

## Who are We?

*So what are the schools like and how do you know if the positive communication concept will work in your school?*

Schumacher's school was a K to 8 elementary school with 150 students and 100 family units. The school had a population of nine teachers in single grade, self contained classrooms, a full time aide in the kindergarten classroom with the kindergarten teacher, and one administrator. No changes to the levels of staffing occurred during the study. The study took place in the fall of 2006. St. Mathew Lutheran School is located in Westland, Michigan. Owned and operated by a Lutheran congregation, the school lies in a suburb west of Detroit.

*Richard W. Schumacher is the Coordinator of Elementary Education at Concordia University in Ann Arbor, Michigan. He holds a Masters Degree in Educational Leadership, earned at Concordia, Ann Arbor. Over the past fourteen years, he has served as a teacher, youth director, and principal at Grace Lutheran School, Kansas City, Kansas, and St. Matthew Lutheran School in Westland, Michigan.*

Salem Lutheran School has an early childhood department of 165 children from age birth through pre-kindergarten. The implementation of "Tell the Teacher More Day" has not yet begun with early childhood families.

Salem School is located in Tomball, Texas, thirty five miles to the northwest of Houston, has a school population of 380 students from grades kindergarten through eight, with 280 family units. There are double grades at each grade level with the exception of grades first and fourth which have three classes. Grades kindergarten through three are basically self contained, however teachers plan together and occasionally share the teaching of various subjects such as science or social studies. Grades four through eight are departmentalized according to the teachers' strengths and certifications. Salem employs twenty four full time faculty, six part time teachers, two administrators and a full time athletic director. Salem is accredited by the National Lutheran School Association in St. Louis, Missouri, and also by the Texas Education Agency through TEPSAC (Texas Private School Accreditation Committee). No changes in staffing occurred at Salem during the implementation of the *Tell the Teacher More Day* positive communication method.

*Currently I serve as the Director of Educational Ministries at Salem Lutheran School. My personal experience involves teaching in both public and parochial educational settings, from early childhood through the university level. I have been in school administration for over twenty years. I have served in the Aldine, Spring, Alief, and Magnolia public school districts, the local community college system and Sam Houston State University as an adjunct professor as well as an administrator at St Matthew Lutheran School in Spring, Texas, and Salem Lutheran School in Tomball.*

*My formal education includes a Bachelors Degree in Speech Pathology and Audiology from the University of Houston, a Masters Degree from Sam Houston State University in Elementary Education, and a Doctorate in Educational Administration from California Coast University.*

The National Lutheran School system is governed through the accreditation process by the division of School Ministries of the Lutheran Church Missouri Synod, St. Louis, Missouri. The Lutheran system is the second largest, nonpublic system in the nation. The synod engages 300,000 students nationwide, from early childhood programs through four year universities.

# Chapter Four

*The Proof that Positive Communication Works!*

*S*o, *if the proof is in the data, then this Tell the Teacher More Day concept really works to create a positive perception of overall school communication.*

Little school, big school, school in Detroit, school in Houston, first concept implemented in 2006, the second implementation in the fall of 2009, the third implementation in the fall of 2010, and the results of the surveys are amazingly similar! To be even more likened to the original concept of "Parents Day," by Mr. Schumacher, I duplicated the survey questions to our school families, with the addition of the question "Did you attend the "Tell the Teacher More Day?" I also wanted the answers to be as unbiased as possible by randomly placing the response options. Both of us sent out surveys in October, after school was in session for the first quarter. The major difference was in the distribution process. I sent out our survey online. (I also titled our day "Tell the Teacher More Day," to be certain that our parents perceived the day was meant for them to do the talking. More details about this later.) Mr. Schumacher's results indicated that forty-six surveys were returned and I had forty-five completed online the first year and 64 completed the survey in 2010. In the following Figures you will read the questions and view the results. The overall analysis will be shared at the end of the Figures.

**What was your impression of the parent teacher meetings on the first day of school (Parents Day/Tell the Teacher More Day)?**

**Figure 4.1.**

| Response | School One 2006 | School Two 2009 | School Two 2010 |
|---|---|---|---|
| Excellent | 53% | 29.3% | 28.3% |
| Beneficial | 34 | 51.2 | 55 |
| Fine | 11 | 9.8 | 10 |
| Not Beneficial | 2 | 7.3 | 5 |
| Waste of Time | 0 | 2.4 | 1.7 |

**Did you enjoy the relaxed atmosphere?**

**Figure 4.2**

| Response | School One 2006 | School Two 2009 | School Two 2010 |
|---|---|---|---|
| Yes | 93% | 88.4% | 91.9 |
| No | 0 | 0 | 0 |
| I Didn't Notice | 5 | 9.3 | 6.5 |
| No Response | 2 | 2.3 | 1.6 |

**Were you better able to connect with your child's teacher versus the teacher addressing the group setting in the past?**

**Figure 4.3**

| Response | School One 2006 | School Two 2009 | School Two 2010 |
|---|---|---|---|
| Yes | 91% | 83.3% | 85.2% |
| No | 7 | 2.4 | 1.6 |
| No Response | 2 | 14.3 | 13.1 |

**Did you feel the teacher listened to you, your questions, and concerns for your child?**

Figure 4.4

| Response | School One 2006 | School Two 2009 | School Two 2010 |
|---|---|---|---|
| Yes | 98% | 83.7% | 88.7% |
| Somewhat | 0 | 11.6 | 8.1 |
| No | 0 | 2.3 | 1.6 |
| No Response | 2 | 2.3 | 1.6 |

**Is Parent's Day/Tell the Teacher More Day something the school should do every year?**

Figure 4.5

| Response | School One 2006 | School Two 2009 | School Two 2010 |
|---|---|---|---|
| Yes | 96% | 92.9% | 93.4% |
| No | 0 | 2.4 | 3.3 |
| No Response | 4 | 4.8 | 3.3 |

**Overall, how would you rate the school when it comes to <u>its effort to communicate with parents?</u>**

**Figure 4.6**

| Response | School One 2006 | School Two 2009 | School Two 2010 |
|---|---|---|---|
| Excellent | 50% | 59.1% | 58.7% |
| Good | 39 | 34.1 | 34.9 |
| Fair | 7 | 6.8 | 6.3 |
| Poor | 2 | 0 | 0 |
| No Response | 2 | 0 | 0 |

**How pleased are you with the school so far?**

**Figure 4.7**

| Response | School One 2006 | School Two 2009 | School Two 2010 |
|---|---|---|---|
| Very Pleased | 61% | 62.2% | 57.8% |
| Pleased | 28 | 20 | 25 |
| Satisfied | 9 | 17.8 | 17.2 |
| Not Satisfied | 0 | 0 | 0 |
| Displeased | 0 | 0 | 0 |
| No Response | 2 | 0 | 0 |

Overall, the data supports the fact that parents were very pleased with the concept of Parent's Day (Tell the Teacher More Day). It is also worth mentioning that those parents who were satisfied, pleased and very pleased (majority) with the schools' attempts at good communication, were also pleased with the way the school year was going so far. The statistics also show a very strong correlation between parent satisfaction and the perception of the school's communication practices (Schumacher, 2006.) This data is also borne out in the survey results from Salem School in 2009 and 2010.

At both schools, parents were required to attend the parent teacher (Tell the Teacher More) meetings by appointment. As with any requirement, a parent or two suggested the meetings be optional. From the overwhelming positive results of the surveys, I see this day as the single most important event to set the stage for positive communication for the rest of the school year. In a forthcoming chapter I will suggest some ways to continue that positive communication throughout the year. Why wouldn't you want to implement this strategy to improve the communication situation with your school parents? The statistics show that school parents will be satisfied as a whole if lines of communication are open and effective. (Schumacher, 2006) Parents want to be heard.

# Chapter Five

## *TELL*
### *"Tell the Teacher More Day"*

*I feel this strategy at the beginning of the school year is the single most effective strategy that leads to positive communication throughout the remainder of the school year.*

Necessary to the success of this day is that it occurs prior to school starting and that every family makes an appointment to meet the teacher. Families with more than one student can then sign up for appointments consecutively. The amount of time should not exceed fifteen minutes. We used our final registration day, when each family comes to school to finalize formal paperwork, choose electives, learn their homeroom teacher's name, etc., to sign up for the parent teacher meetings. Parents were also provided with a "Tell the Teacher More" form to take with them to complete and bring back for their appointment (see below).

"Tell the Teacher More Day" was considered to be a regular school day, just like our two annual parent teacher conference days. Teachers were content to know that it was not another addition to their already very busy schedule before school starts. The teacher's role in these meetings is to listen, ask for clarification if necessary, and to make the event as positive and beneficial as possible.

Since teachers had another opportunity to talk with the parents and students as a group during the before-school orientation meetings, this setting is not for explaining classroom rules, format, or providing a syllabus. This time is solely for communication- and the teacher's major role is to listen, not talk. Teachers are instructed to redirect parents should the discussion go toward classroom topics.

Once inside the building, the school personnel provided assistance finding classrooms, especially for the new families. Teachers were asked to provide a home made snack or dessert to add to the friendly discussion. In the classroom, teachers were asked to provide adult size chairs and arrange them in an area of the room that was attractive and informal. If it was the nature of the teacher to not stay on schedule, then the teacher would set a timer to keep the discussion on track and on time. (We do this for parent teacher conferences also.)

To help collect consistent and valuable information, the parents had the form to complete prior to their appointment. This helped the teacher enormously instead of having to drive the conversation or take notes constantly. (Again, giving full attention to the parents' comments regarding their child so to add to the purpose of the meeting.) The form was then surrendered to the teacher. The most important information to gather was the best way in which to communicate with the parents.

*In preparing the "Tell the Teacher More" form, I felt it necessary to stay away from characteristic labels such as strengths and weaknesses (nouns) and sought words that were instead behavior descriptors (adjectives). The parent responses appeared more positive and less judgmental.*

### Tell The Teacher More .....

**Child's Name**          **Nickname?**

**Describe the family dynamics....**
**Describe your child's temperament...**
**What motivates your child?**
**What distresses your child?**
**What concerns do you have that you want the teacher to know?**
**\*\*\*\*\*What's the best way to communicate with you, the parent?\*\*\*\*\***
**What else would you like your child's teacher to know?**

## What the teachers had to say about Tell the Teacher More Day...

*"Loved it! It really gave me a chance to attend the needs of the student with the parent one on one. We had a great foundation before the school year even began."*

*"Great way to connect with the parents. It opened the lines of communication. Excellent way to start the year."*

*"I thought it was helpful to meet the parents and know the family dynamics. I always wished I had a face to with then name so I could make an association right away!"*

*"It was nice forming a relationship with the parents before school started. It also provided insight concerning the child. I think it made the whole year start on a positive note."*

*"I personally was very excited about this project! I have done home visits and a meet the teacher night in the past but it always seemed to be a huge time commitment and a safety concern for the home visits and the meet the teacher night was overwhelming because you aren't able to carry on a solid conversation with so many parents and students in and out of the classroom during an allotted time period. "*

*"I am a teacher that wants to know as much as I can about my students so that I can identify their strengths and weaknesses right off the bat and help them out. I do not want to see them struggle, and if knowing a bit more about their school life and their outside home life at the beginning of the year is going to help me to do that than I am all for it!"*

*"I thought is was a great opportunity to learn about the kids and meet the family, which I always like to do at the beginning of the year. It is a very proactive approach to establishing a positive relationship with the family."*

*"On a very positive note, by having this meeting it eliminated all the "hallway" mini-meetings the first few days of school.*

*Example: Please seat my child in the front; You know Bob is good friends with Steve, please seat them together; Sally is on medication, she needs to go to the nurse at 10 am; most of which you forgot because you were in the hallway and had no way to write it down!*

"*Some parents came into the meeting expecting me to do all the talking. They were very surprised when I sat back and just waited for them to "tell me..."*

"*Another thought- I did NOT hear any parents complain, but being pro-active, I felt badly that the parents had to come up to school for registration, orientation, and "Tell the Teacher More." Maybe this is not a bad thing, but should we try to combine them? However, as a teacher, I liked the fact that we did not have to try to do these outside of the school day or after school or spread over 2 or 3 days. I liked the fact that a day was set aside to do this.*"

"*I don't know how to do this, but for those grades that have several teachers in addition to the home room teacher, it would be great for all the teachers to be at the meeting. However, scheduling it could be a nightmare and overwhelming for the parents!*"

"*Some parents are not as talkative as others and so I would have to ask questions to help get the info from them. Others have written a three to four page report and we have to narrow it down.*"

*"You can't foresee what types of issues will come up during the year. No matter how good a relationship is, some parents react like "mother bears protecting their young" when they perceive a problem."*

*"Mostly it helped me to match/remember the kids with the parents and the family situation so I did appreciate the meetings."*

*"Could other days be consolidated? We are asking parents to take off work 3 different days before school starts."*

*"Some parents do not fully disclose, and I ended up finding things out later in the year that should have been addressed the year before, but weren't."*

*"Sometimes too much time is spent rehashing last year's problems. New year- new beginning."*

*"At first I was skeptical about how effective this strategy would be. I wasn't sure how honest parents would be about their children."*

*"Great idea! The first meeting was casual and positive."*

*"It was a good way to "break the ice," hear a few things about their child and connect names and faces. Some came with a lot written down and others with very little. The same was true for the actual meetings. Some parents naturally talk more and share more."*

When Mr. Schumacher and I visited following Salem's first implementation of *Tell the Teacher More Day,* we shared the unexpected outcome of teachers knowing who the parents are on the very first day of school, rather than taking well into the school year to become familiar with names and faces. In addition, the students witnessed the friendly interactions of their parents with their teacher from the very first day of school.

# Chapter Six

## *TELL*

*Engage in the best avenue of
communication for each family.*

**P**erhaps the most difficult part of any initiative is to
follow through with it. This is especially true when all
is not going along perfectly. Following through with the
ways in which parents want to be informed and involved can
be overwhelming. It helps to reflect that as parents we are
tempted to live our lives through the lives of our children.
We have only the memories of our own school days on
which to rely, so we could very well be still working through
childhood feelings psychologically or emotionally.

Of course parents want only the best for their children.
The problem occurs when getting the A is more important
than grasping what hard work it takes to get one. Or that a
grade of B is perfectly respectable when it's earned with the
best effort. In this day and age of instant gratification (I like
to refer to this as drive-through grace), this attitude could
be referred to as entitlement. Teachers and administrators

find themselves in a very precarious situation as we desire to both please parents, but also to teach our students that learning should be challenging and that only hard work and self –discipline earn good grades.

"Our first job is to teach. But that doesn't mean we function in a vacuum. Teaching means many things – including dealing with academics and being sensitive to where children are in the process. It includes caring, encouraging, praising progress, and helping students always do better. Along with necessities, we need to function out of a "sense of community" with other school personnel." (DeBruyn,1999.) DeBruyn continues to write, "Once we open the school and classroom doors…we need to move into the larger community that involves parents…too much goes on in a good classroom these days for it to be regarded as an isolation ward…we should develop a partnership (with parents) out of desire –not because it's the law. After all, the children in our classes are more than just our students- they are their parents' children. And the education of these children is a *shared* responsibility. This must be our professional stance. Therefore, we do not have the right to exclude parents –when things are going well or when they're going badly."

*Following are the teacher responses as to* **"whether it was easier to approach parents after the initial meeting"** *(Tell the Teacher More Day) follow -*

*"Yes. I had information about strengths and weaknesses from the parents' viewpoint, knew their expectations for the child, and the best way to communicate with each family, which set the groundwork for future meetings. Meeting before school begins takes away the first time meeting "jitters." Parents were more at ease having talked once, and were willing to come in for conferences on a regular basis. I was able to use testing, classroom work and observation, as well as information from the initial meeting to setup plans for each child, communicate those to the parents, and have more at home support."*

*"Having already established a relationship with the parents made it much easier. I have a student with a severe behavior disorder. When problems arose I felt very comfortable talking to the parents."*

Sample of actual email-

Dear (parent)

Just wanted to let you know that L had a good day today. I have been concerned with L's emotional well being recently, as she has had a tough couple of weeks.

Se had two meltdowns in the last two weeks, in which I had to call the nurse to remove her from the classroom, and then the two incidents at the end of last week where she ran away from me, once in the middle school hallway during class, and once outside on the playground. I have been working hard with her to try and regain her composure when she feels she is losing it. I have been keeping Dr. G informed of the situation. I am excited with C's involvement with L. She seems to respond to her and is motivated by her program. I pray this is the tool L needs to control herself. But by the same token I am concerned for L and must keep the classroom needs a priority as well. I have discussed this with Dr. G and we agree that if L has another emotional outburst that she should go back to ½ days. Her emotional disruptions make it challenging for the students and me. And her running away puts me in a very precarious position. Without a doubt I want L to succeed. Hopefully, with our continued support, we can give L the tools she needs to thrive. Blessings in Christ,

Dear (teacher)

Thank you for the update. We, too, are concerned about L's behavior. We agree with and support the plan for her to attend half days if she has another meltdown.

We want for L, you, and the other students to have a calm and safe learning environment. We are also very pleased with the work CL and the staff are doing with L. For whatever reason, L has formed a strong attachment to CL. We will continue to work with them to help L make good decisions regarding her behavior and to practice self-control...once again, thank you, both you and Dr. G, for working so hard with us to get L on a good, straight path.

*"Definitely. I felt like the parent and I were on the same side!"*

*"Yes."* Meeting with the parents one on one helped *"break the ice"* before the school year started. It also helped me to be able to pick my parents out of all the parents in the entire school! It assisted in building a communication system as well so that the parents felt we cared for their child and would use the information to help understand their child better before he/she stepped into our classroom.

*"Yes. "* The first meeting being a positive one is always helpful. When I hear from the parent what they see as a child's weakness and when it is addressed later in the year it doesn't come as such a surprise."

*"After the first meeting we have a better understanding of each other's personalities."*

*"Yes. You get rid of the initial nerves of meeting for the first time over a sensitive issue."*

*"Yes. They knew the expectations so it was easier when I called to say their child wasn't doing his or her part."*

*"Yes. Those parents that were straight forward in the meeting*

*held nothing back and so when conflicts arose, it seemed easier to deal with. The reverse was also true."*

*"Yes. After meeting with Mr. and Mrs. ___, I was able to identify them in the hallway and speak to them about some initial classroom behavior I had observed in their son."*

*"Yes. It was clear that many wanted to be kept "in the loop" about any and all problems their child might be having. This made it easier to ask for a short school conference early in the year to nip any potential problems in the bud."*

*"Yes. Most of the time. However, it is never easy to bring up a difficult topic or behavior problem. Plus, some parents do not fully disclose various information. Example: some parents defend their child's behavior with "excuses" or blaming it on others so it is difficult to approach them. Also, when a teacher is not informed that a student is on medication, when the behavior changes, a discussion about this is not an option."*

*"Yes. Sharing certain information made me have insight onto both the child and her at home situation."*

*"Yes and No. In some instances, from the initial parent meeting I learned "a bit of information about the child. So, if she purposely forgets to bring books home so she doesn't have to study, I could inform the parent about what was happening and have her check her backpack before leaving that day. On the other hand, some topics are not pleasant to bring up like stealing, bullying, etc. these meetings are just hard."*

*"Yes. Personal emails about family issues and social issues were just easier to share and follow up on." (Sample emails will be shard in a later chapter.)*

Sample of actual email-

Dear (parent)

What happened to A? I saw he and dad walking up the pathway, but they never came in and then they left? I had ordered his lunch, but told them he never came in so you will not be charged. I hope all is well.

Dear (teacher)

We had a late night last night. My husband felt A's backpack and did not feel a water bottle or a snack. I failed to communicate to him what I had emailed you. He thought he was dropping A off without lunch snack or water. He was in a hurry, so he just put A in the truck and drove off. I did not find out until lunch time. Major communication breakdown....

You can assume from these responses that the overwhelming result was yes, the initial "Tell the Teacher More Day" made a positive impact on future communication.

Of course, we would be somewhat superhuman (or subhuman?) creatures should we feel delivering bad news about a student were made easier. It's the fact that we already have an idea about who the parents are, how and what they want communicated and that we are partners in the education of their child that really matters. Now let's see how the communication improved due to the initial positive tone set at "Tell the Teacher More Day."

# Chapter Seven

## TELL
*Listen without defense to the parent.*
*Confrontation can lead to fear for*
*both teachers and parents.*

Remember the comment from the teacher that her concerns about a parent were sucking the joy out of her teaching? The feelings are still raw and the "lump in the throat" still occurs for many of us who have received a message saying that a parent needs to speak with us "right away" and that he or she "sounded angry." We may feel a need to be defensive even if it's just because the reason the parent needs to meet is unknown. It's normal to be anxious, but we can control our defensiveness. "There isn't any reason for you, as a teacher, to fear a parent conference. But there might be a reason for you to feel guilty – if a student's behavior or academic performance was such that you should have notified the parents before they telephoned you...if the parents and/or teacher build up negative feelings prior to the conference, the meeting itself will fall somewhat, if not completely, short of success. When teacher-parent conferences fail, student problems are not solved; they are multiplied." (DeBruyn, 1999.)

*Since listening intently to the parents talk about their child and gleaning information as to how they wanted to be communicated with concerning their child's progress was a priority, did the positive communication that began with "Tell the Teacher More Day" continue? See the teacher responses below-*

*"I have taken (student) under my wing. She is a wonderful child from a wonderful family that struggles to make ends meet. Mom and I have worked to make her year a great one. We continue to work as a team. I look forward to having her brother next year."*

*"Actually, it depends on what needed to be communicated throughout the year, or whether it was resolved. Example: one student has attention difficulties. Until the child can "attend" better, the child cannot attend well to any large group instruction. Since the behavior hasn't changed, it is difficult to keep talking about it and/or expect any other outcome when speaking to parents."*

*"Yes. It made the second conference a time when we could discuss more specifics instead of just meeting and getting to know each other. With each consecutive conference, I feel I can know and understand the parents and their opinions better."*

*"Yes. It is easy to email the parent when the student has had an off day. It's wonderful to have a face with a name. I have exchanged many positive and negative emails with parents over the course of the year. I am freer to express myself via email since I know them."*

Samples of actual emails-

Dear (parent)

Hi. Just a note to let you know that _____has a Spanish test next Thursday. Please have him study all vocabulary in Chapter 2 and pay special attention to subject pronouns page 87 and "ar" verbs pages 90 and 91. He really needs to study for this.

Dear (teacher)

Thank you for letting us know. We will have him study over the weekend. We appreciate you help.

Dear (parent)

B has passed his Spanish with a 76 this nine weeks but I know he is capable of a much better grade. We have our first test of the 4th quarter on Tuesday. His most recent quiz grades were 61 and 3. The low quiz grades tell me that he does not know the information. Spanish can be difficult and requires study and practice in class. I am hoping that he will study all of chapter 3 this weekend, and move his grade in a better direction this last nine weeks. Parent/Teacher conferences are April 6th. I invite you to come. I can share more in person than I can I email.

Dear (teacher)

B would like to stay after school on Monday if you are available. Please let me know if that works. Thank you.

Dear (parent)

I can use some volunteer help with stapling books together. Please let me know.

Dear (teacher)

I will staple the books!

Dear (teacher)

Oops! I forgot to send them today .I will try for tomorrow. The cupcake thing was a disaster! I had misplaced our valentines and just remembered there were 16 kids in the class –so I sent 17 cakes. I didn't know about the new kid. I do now!

I feel terrible! C is really happy this year and it should be said from time to time! We do appreciate how kind and loving you are with the kids. C really feels special in your class. C does very well when he feels loved at school.

*Email communication has increased in frequency from last year. Parents tell me they appreciate it because students "don't tell them anything." I still visit with parents in the hall – since we had a friendly start it makes the mini conferences easier and faster."*

*"My communication with parents has been good all year."*

*"I talk to and send emails daily. One parent with whom I met at the beginning of the year still seemed to have her guard up. As the year went on, we've built a strong relationship. At this point, we talk or email daily."*

*"Yes. I have had more communication with all families this year. Many will ask questions as they pick up, some will call with their questions and some will email me.*
*I have only two families where communication has remained at a low level. I have used phone calls or asking after school for a meeting as my main communication this year. I feel that those students with learning difficulties, who have had low benchmark scores, or needed more than just a classroom approach have been better served this year by the number of conferences held with parents."*

*"Yes. Parents realize that I have their child's best interests in mind."*
*"All parent complaints are accompanied with a $5 bill! (humor here)*
*"All positive communications are free."*
*"We have great parents at Salem!"*

*"Yes. I feel I have been able to honestly approach the parents, even when it is something about their child they may not like to hear (such as a behavior issue or lack of effort/studying to prepare.) It helped that I stressed to parents we are a team and have a partnership in their child's education together."*

*"I think as the year progressed parents saw that the website was updated often. Class emails were sent if a major event was coming. They heard or received quick turn around on emails and phone calls. My point being they felt very comfortable coming and giving me important or not so important information- fyi, Sally may be tired, we got home late or yes, we are going to have Dan tested. I have paperwork for you to fill out. I don't have anything to document other than feelings, but this year I spend more time sending and returning email/phone calls than before. Also, updating the webpage."*

Without a doubt, listening to parents and following up with them as to the progress of their child, has yielded obvious positive results. Master Teacher/author, Robert L. DeBruyn (1999), refers to the listening skills teachers need to hone as an "attitude." Once achieved, parents will count listening as a great strength. Unfortunately, without the right attitude, we can be perceived as unapproachable.

DeBruyn lists three specific techniques: eye contact with the speaker, engaging the speaker physically (leaning toward the speaker), and responsive listening (repeating in your own words what the person is saying to you.) Responsive listening is without a doubt the most difficult skill to hone because it requires the most of you- really listening and engaging to what the parent is saying. Perhaps this is the area as teachers we fail first. We need to be empathetic and place our own opinion, advice, and correction aside and really listen. Then "parents will believe we are easy to talk to, and will communicate more easily and freely with us." (DeBruyn, 1999).

One last piece of advice while employing these listening techniques according to Debruyn is that the attitude in general should reflect warmth. Concentrate on what really matters- the child. Show genuine concern. Debruyn concludes "a cold, hasty or matter-of –fact-attitude will not secure the trust and confidence of any human being. Sometimes we think these attitudes prove our objectivity and professionalism. Nothing could be further from the truth. The image you project as a teacher and as a human being reflects upon you, your teaching, and your entire school."

This past summer I met with three different parents willing to share concerns with me before the school year begins. In all three cases the issue was around communication. When I asked the parents why they had not come to me sooner, they all stated that the education their child was receiving was acceptable.

It was the communication with the teacher that wasn't going well. They wanted to be certain that their expectations would be met over the next school year. We discussed how important *Tell the Teacher More Day* would become.

# Chapter Eight

## *TELL*

*Lead as the professional! In the educational arena, the teacher is the professional. If schools were hospitals, teachers would be the doctors. They would be diagnosing, treating, adjusting, monitoring progress, etc. Indeed, teachers are the professionals.*

As the professionals, then, teachers need to take the lead in communicating with parents. Statistics from the parent surveys after the first quarter of school indicated that parents will be more satisfied as a whole if the lines of communication are open and effective. The benefits for the teacher is simple: happy parents are far easier to work with then those who are displeased. So, if issues arise, whether academic or behavioral, wouldn't it be beneficial to communicate with the parents sooner, rather than later?

Why is it that teachers are reluctant to go to parents with problems and that parents are reluctant to ask teachers if there is a problem? Parents and teachers need to be proactive in their communication and stay regularly informed as to student progress. Parents deserve regular updates concerning their child's academic and behavioral status. By providing regular updates, the teacher continues the rapport- building process well into the school year, having begun it on a positive note with the conversation at "Tell the Teacher More Day."

Another benefit of the parent survey indicated to us that parents view overall satisfaction with the school and school communication in the same light. Parents like to have information concerning their children. If the teacher is the professional, then the teacher shall take the lead by finding many and varied ways to communicate with parents in the best way possible as indicated to the teacher at "Tell the Teacher More Day." The teacher must be the leader in the year long process of communicating with the parents.

Additionally, the school administrator must actively support the teachers to make parent communication a priority. By helping to establish a climate of relationship-building between the school office and parents as well, the administrator models positive communication for the entire school community.

Finally, parents must do their part in this collaboration toward positive communication. They too have to commit to communicate openly and honestly and in a respectful manner with the teacher.

It is here that I want to share with you three specific emails that I feel are excellent examples of the teacher taking the lead as the professional in the communication exchange-


**To the Teacher –**

**Me Again** ☺

A is not communicating w/me very well since I haven't been home all week. I've been taking care of my husband's grandmother. So, I'm begging you for help to answer my questions. What is the response to chapter 9 and page 15 questions? What book or books are needed to redo these? Can A bring those books home to study this weekend? If so, please send them with him.

I can get the vocab #10 online and we can look over those this weekend and he can retake it on Monday..in class or before school starts? He will be there by 7:30 on Monday. I have no idea what the beaver quiz is or to how to help him to study. Sorry. I'm a little lost. Its so hard pulling stuff out of him over the phone. By the way, I'm having gastric bypass surgery on Monday, so if he seems to be acting a little strange that day that's probably why. Just wanted to give you a heads up.

Thank you –

*Mary Beth Gaertner, Ed.D.*

## To the Parent –

**Congratulations on the gastric bypass! That is too cool. My dad has had one and has been happy with the results for years. If you would like to email me a list of things you'd like for A to fix or makeup, I will make sure he does them this Thursday. The librarian has offered to administer late work to anyone that needs it. Let m know. Good luck! I'll be praying for you.**

## And another-

## To the Teacher-

**I am very disappointed to receive your email this morning re: the grading of this test – I felt certain you would say some mistake in grading had been made. I must tell you that I cannot believe his grade went down to a C simply because he forgot the labels. While I understand that labels should count for something and they must learn to add this detail, it is preposterous for him to end up with an 84 when he demonstrated complete mastery of the skill being tested... I am very upset about this and do not plan to accept this grade as a fair assessment of the content being tested. I look forward to haearing back from you regarding this issue.**

To the Parent –

I am sorry that you are disappointed in my answer. I took the time this afternoon to talk with two upper grade math teachers at Salem. They also take off points for a label on a problem-solving question. Please remember to look at the big picture. This is one test grade out of many this quarter. H currently has a 94 in math class and is doing great! If you would like to discuss this further, we can set up a meeting with me and the math department head. Have a great evening!

One more –

To the Parent-

I have heard in the last day some information in regards to R's absence from Salem. I would appreciate it if you would contact myself, Mrs. W, or Dr. G and let us know officially what the status is on R continuing at Salem. If he is no longer attending, I would like your advice on what needs to be done with the supplies and materials that are currently in his locker and desk. On a more personal note, I am hoping that all is well with you. When we met with Mrs. W and myself a couple of weeks ago, you alluded to some inner struggles, and that has concerned both myself and Mrs. W.

Waiting to hear from you –

## To the Teacher-

Thanks for your concern. R is fine we had to make changes that was best for all of us our money problems have been hard but during Easter week we decided to start doing things different I will make sure all is books are returned to school. I was going to try a home school group from our church but decided R needs more that they can offer he is back at TISD. It was just the right thing to do for everything. I know things are going to get better I am looking forward to that.

Thanks.

***Let's see, then, how the teachers have responded to ways to what additional strategies we can implement as a school to approach positive communication with parents?***

*"Could implement a Facebook page for Salem"*

*"Communication has always been open, honest, and direct. I find that works best for me. I am not one to beat around the bush but I try to do in a loving way- just as I want to be talked to by my child's teacher."*

*"I liked what we did. I liked knowing the parents and becoming informed about their child. It took a shorter time to get to the students. It was easier to talk with parents after the first meeting."*

*"I think we already have quite a few- the new meet the teacher before school began, email and websites for general information and comments, phone calls, conferences, all school events and open houses — all of those promote communication and relationship."*

*"One thing that I have done in the past, but takes time is notify the parents via email or a phone call if a student drops below a 70 percent in my class. This seemed to work well, and really perk up their grades. I also would continue to encourage our parents to check the website- its packed full of information!"*

*"At the beginning of the year we showed parents how to go to the website and how to use the different pages. Think this was very helpful for the parents who were present. I did hear some*

*parents talking about it in the hall – "if you were at orientation, you would know how to get to the calendar."* ☺ *So, for next year, we may want to pick a different topic- how to access the science book online."*

*"As far as emails- trying to take a positive turn/spin on every situation, helping parents see the big picture, suggestions that will help their child and most of all that I love their child! Thank them for their partnership in their child's education.*

*"I feel it's imperative that teachers have their class email lists and phone numbers."*

*Emailing and calling parents is the most effective form of communication for me."*

*What we have done so far is excellent! Very different (in a good way) from past years."*

*"My suggestion would be to make a concerted effort to contact the parent when their child does something good."*

*"I have been trying to have face to face meetings with all families."*

*"Anything resembling a "happy note." A quick comment at the door about how excited a child was to learn about rocks, for example. Or just saying to the parent," Johnny did an outstanding job on math today," or "Susie told the class about her vacation and she did a great job organizing her thoughts."*

*"Keeping parent updated on upcoming events. Smiling teachers who have a positive attitude."*

*"Be approachable."*

*"Have a meet and greet day to meet all parents. Maybe this is middle school specific. Some of the issues I had are not with my home room students."*

*From a parent survey…*
*"The only improvement I see that needs to be made is to have a more personal relationship with the home room teacher. I did not receive any correspondence from the home room teacher. I believe this is the only area lacking that is in need of improvement."*

# Chapter Nine

## Conclusions

We think we finally found a vehicle to help us as educators to establish a positive climate for communication with parents –*Tell the Teacher More Day*. The keys to its success include raising the value of attendance to include all parents and the depth of implementation by all of the teachers. For us, we informed the parents three times -in print via an email update about back to school activities, at the time of final registration parents were asked to make their individual appointments, and then at family orientation, parents heard about the importance from me the day before *Tell the Teacher More Day* was to take place. I stated more than once that *Tell the Teacher More Day* "was the single most important day parents would have to communicate with their child's teacher about the needs of their child and their own expectations as to the preferred method of communication."

A few parents did not attend and appointments were scheduled with them at the teacher's invitation. The teachers were asked to prepare a home made snack, create a warm atmosphere, and keep the appointments to fifteen minutes while staying on track through the use of the form provided to parents for completion prior to the appointment. If parents wandered from discussing their child they were directed back to the focus.

Teachers had been instructed in the implementation of "responsive listening" and based upon my personal observations that day, were applying those techniques. I sat at the school front desk for the major part of the day and asked parents as they were leaving how their appointments went, and every parent I asked responded positively.

Before school officially started we saw the families three times – final registration day, family orientation day (where the students met the teachers and visited the classrooms), and *Tell the Teacher More Day*. Registration was come- and-go, and family orientation times were offered both during the day and in the evening so that working parents were not forced to miss work. Appointments for *Tell the Teacher More Day* were at the parent's discretion and were scheduled early in the morning and into the evening to accommodate parents as necessary. School started the next day- and ended at noon so everyone went home on a positive note, and to get the jitters out!

Communication has increased significantly on all levels- electronically and face to face. Parents are asking questions when they don't understand something and teachers are more confident to contact the parent quickly when they notice the student struggling.

As administrators we have asked to be "cc'd" on any

parent communication so that we have a total picture of the scope of school communication, not just those messages that would be considered serious or troublesome.

Parents were told of this strategy so not to be surprised or questioning why we were included. What a difference! What a load of emails! (I receive about 75-100 emails per day, half of which I am "cc'd.") Rather than being included only in communication where potential problems are being addressed, we are also now aware of the specific compliments and regular daily and weekly communication that is taking place. When we receive emails from parents as administrators, we "cc" the teacher or teachers involved in our responses to the parents also- to embrace accountability on all our parts and to promote transparency to the parents in terms of communication. Due to all the time spent on campus before school started, it is easier to call parents by name and address them when they arrive at school in the morning or when picking up in the afternoon because we know them.

Granted, it has taken a concerted effort to get to this point. I can't imagine going back to the prior ways of doing things. Whenever focused on a target like positive communication, opportunities will come to test it. We do our best to listen and learn and respond with clarity and in a positive tone to our parents. Always. We are the professionals. We have a service to deliver and we know parents have a choice. But the best reason to invest in positive communication is because we have children in our midst. If they are to become the leaders of tomorrow- a multi-faceted, global, technological world - then they will need to have been mentored in those very face to face skills that cannot be taught through the use of technology or by socializing online.

Responsive listening, nonverbal communication, and simple eye contact will need to be modeled and practiced.

Parents will always be their child's most impactful influence, and as long as students are still learning in classrooms, teachers will be the second most important. We finally found a way to partner successfully with parents, to discover their expectations, and to wow them- by talking with them about their children! We found the Way to Go!

# References:

## Chapter One

Mathew 18: 15. *"If your brother sins against you, go and show him his fault, just between the two of you."* Zondervan Publishing House.

## Chapter Two

Schumacher, R. (2007) *Bridging the Communication Gap: The Value of Intentional Positive Teacher-Initiated Communication.* (Available from the Lutheran Education Journal Volume 142, No 2. 104-125.)

Ames,C., Khou, M., &Watkins, T. (1993). *Parent Involvement: the relationship between school-to-home communication and parents' perceptions and beliefs. (Available from the ERIC Document REpordiction Service No. ED 362-271).*

Barrera, J. M., & Warner, L. (2006). *Involving families in school evens.* Kappa Delta Pi Record, 42(2). 72-75.

Freytag, C. E. (2001). *Teacher-parent communication: starting the year off right.* (Available from the ERIC Document Reproduction Service No. ED 460 087).

Upham, D. A., Cheney. D., & Manning, B. (1998). *What do teachers and parents want in their communication patterns?* Middle School Journal 29(5). 48-55.

Warner, L. (2002). *Family involvement: A key component of student and school success.*
(Available from the ERIC Document Reproduction Service No. ED 470 319).

Witmer, M. M. (2005). *The fourth r in education – relationships.* The Clearing House.
78(5). 224-228.

## Chapter Six

DeBruyn, R., (1999). *Understanding and Relating to Parents …Professionally.* The MASTER Teacher, Inc. Manhattan, Kansas

CPSIA information can be obtained at www.ICGtesting.com
Printed in the USA
BVOW08s1148050515

399018BV00001B/3/P